# *Food for Thought*

## MARGARET MUNNERLYN

© 2010, Margaret Munnerlin

All Rights Reserved

No parts of the book may be recreated in any form without the expressed written consent of: Tony Bean, Darren Shell, Weuffer Daffer Productions, and Fideli Publishing, Inc.

ISBN: 978-1-60414-273-0

Library of Congress Number: 2003098542

Published by
**Fideli Publishing, Inc.**

## Table of Contents

"TOMORROW" ............................................................................ 1
"IMPORTANT" ............................................................................ 2
"MISTAKE" ................................................................................ 3
"LIFE" ........................................................................................ 4
"INSECURITY" ........................................................................... 5
"THE FOOL" .............................................................................. 6
"THE GIVE" ............................................................................... 7
"YOU" ........................................................................................ 8
"MISTER INSPIRATION" .......................................................... 9
"IN-TOUCH" ............................................................................ 10
"THE CHILD" ........................................................................... 11
"BEHAVIOR" ........................................................................... 13
"BEING SUCCESSFUL" .......................................................... 15
"THE SUN ALSO RISES" ........................................................ 18
"VISTORS ON PLANET EARTH" ........................................... 21
"THE SPIRIT" .......................................................................... 23
"TIME" ..................................................................................... 26
"ALL EXPERIENCES" ............................................................ 28
"ONE TEAR" ........................................................................... 29

| | |
|---|---|
| "FRIENDSHIP" | 30 |
| "BEAUTY" | 31 |
| "WEIGHT" | 33 |
| "LAZY" | 35 |
| "FINDING YOUR WAY" | 36 |
| "LOVE" | 38 |
| "MONEY" | 40 |
| "MA-GEORGIE" | 42 |
| "A LISTENER" | 43 |
| "MAMA AND DEAR" | 44 |
| "GRANDMA AND PAPA" | 46 |
| "EILEEN" | 48 |
| "ROBYN" | 49 |
| "ANN-MARIE" | 50 |
| "ARNETIA-SPECIAL" | 51 |
| "ASABERRY" | 52 |
| WUNAND-"GOD IS GOOD" | 53 |
| "A HIGHER POWER" | 54 |
| About The Author | 55 |

# "TOMORROW"

Tomorrow, what about tomorrow? Who does it belong too? Is it yours, is it mine? Can we reserve, preserve or appoint ourselves for tomorrow? What is tomorrow? Tomorrow is a mystery. Who's to say I claim it? We are not able to live the future today nor are we able to retrieve yesterday except in our minds. Today or part of today is all we have, however, today will soon be yesterday and tomorrow will soon be today.

## "IMPORTANT"

We see ourselves as important. We are so important being important that we have lost sight of what is really important the creator or the creation? Would you say that something that is created is more important than the creator? Is the fruit worth more than its seeds? Has man ever made a seed, a raindrop, a clear day or a dark night? Is it true that man can only make something from something that already exist? Why then are we not humble and appreciative. Do we think because something exist it must exist? Let us put importance where it rightfully belongs with the creator.

## "MISTAKE"

One of the most misused words in the dictionary is the word mistake. In most cases we should be saying the word embarrassed or caught because we are sorry for nothing but being found out. For example, had not the secret been discovered it's very likely the story would have never been told. If we think before we speak and when we speak, not to undermine the listener's intelligence we would save ourselves embarrassment.

# "LIFE"

We always talk about, sing about and try to live love through the fantasy of reality and call it life.  Life's reality seems to be a difficult concept for humans to deal with.  The organization of society makes the icing which is the illusion more relevant than the cake which is the truth more acceptable.  We are so conditioned to the illusion that it is virtually impossible to look at any aspect of life without rose colored glasses.  Unless we begin to call a spade a spade there is no possibility of positive change in any aspect of life.  Change only comes about when change is seen as necessary and it is not necessary if what we do is thought of as good for those that benefit.

## "INSECURITY"

The dictionary defines insecurity as showing fear unable to make safe decisions and having poor judgment. When a man displays insecurity he cheats lies and holds anyone else responsible for his own misbehavior excusing it as right. Women are more overt with their feelings and voices. It is dangerous to deceive because in the end the deceiver loses. Do yourself a favor and be straight with those you say, you care for because if you do not respect and love will be no more than an illusive fantasy of what might have been.

## "THE FOOL"

The fool would like you to believe that

life outside of his or her realm is an

infinitely hopeless course.  The idiot is not

capable of making oneself understood or

of understanding and must be told repeatedly.

The imbecile never masters anything but functions

mechanically (Just enough to get by).

The moron can learn but refuses to

work independently without

regressing.  The simpleton moves with the

wave sees nothing and feels everything.

## "THE GIVE"

The power of the give, it was already given

before we gave it?  What is the give?

Can you see it, no!  Only the effects of it

but you know its there.  We all have it,

and what's more important is using it.  What

is it?  The gift of the give the contract

is God's and the tool is ours.  The true beauty

is consciously or unconsciously it never stops!

## "YOU"

Many people see it or feel it

and short-change their whole-self.

Your cautiousness and your ounce-of-prevention

approach could better serve you

without most of the stress if you would put

more confidence in the decisions you make,

just be a little more chancy and by that

I do not mean to throw caution to the wind

overall, I feel you are one who tries very

hard and I admire and respect that.

Guess who this is!

## "MISTER INSPIRATION"

Mister inspiration, you have brought out in me things that have been locked-up over a long period of time. I've taken a moment to think and reach back into the gold of my mind and come up with a "pure gem" shaped it, molded it and looked at the finished product from the outside in, to see the radiance and it feels good! Inspiration is the key to success and success is born of sweat.

## "IN-TOUCH"

Get in-touch with you. We keep. trying to get others to get us happy, successful and so-called fulfilled. This kind of thinking does not work because until you get in-touch with you others can not share happy, successful or fulfillment; they can only help and share you, with you.

Think about it!

## "THE CHILD"

How long do our children belong to us? I guess it's all according to how you want them to belong to you. We the fathers give them life, we the mothers suffer to bring that life into the world; together fathers and mothers feed our children physically, mentally and emotionally, helping to bring them through the empty mindedness that life has welcome them with.

During their growth toward maturity they
need us in a dependent way however, the
stronger their minds and hearts become the
less dependent they are on us although, our
children will always belong to us but, in an
independent assertive kind of way their growth
is also our growth. We learn that the word
"belong" is not the word we want
to use we want to use the word apart
of or an extension of us
because in reality we all belong to
society.

## "BEHAVIOR"

Behavior is tied-up with the environment we are reared in and socialized in. We learn early on how to behave. In most cases we accept this information without question and those of us that rebel against accepting information from authority for the sake of authority are thought of as being different and different being thought of as something bad.

Behavior is subjective and passive making it pliable to blank suggestions by others or its questioning and objective, refusing to take at face value opinions and directions of others. Unfortunately, and generally, we have not been allowed or encouraged to be independent thinkers and as a result we go through life as dependent passive followers from the cradle to the grave and generation to generation; this behavior stays true unless we make the necessary changes.

## "BEING SUCCESSFUL"

Massively, there are more failures than successful people and in general, the reason for it is a self-defeatist attitude. Be it parental influences or peer pressure failure is more prominent than drug addiction. To acquire success you must be humble, persistent and analytical of your ability and of how much risk you are willing to take and not be thin skinned.

First, be willing to accept failure and use each failure as a spring-board on the road to success. For example, do not think of failure as "all is lost" instead learn from those experiences to do better, swallow that foolish pride and be flexible. Second, "never say die," be repetitious until success is yours. Third, think of what you did or did not do to succeed (be honest) and make positive changes that will lead to your success.

In conclusion, do not allow others to say or infer negative mental vibes that will surely contribute greatly to your failure. Let their unproductive comments roll off your back as if they were water. The initial step is always the hardest but repetition will reward you in the end.

# "THE SUN ALSO RISES"

The sun also rises, death comes, birth comes and the sun also rises, we are born, we travel life's road; death comes and life comes again, but the sun also rises. Children play, man builds, woman cares, but the sun also rises.

We cry, we laugh, there's pain, there's pleasure, but the sun also rises. The dark airless, dry environment is our death, inherited from Adam, but the sun also rises. This light, air and water that has been extended to us, are our engine to life. Nothing has, and no one can stop what is and what will be, and the sun also rises.

Don't worry about life because life is not worried about you. Life is on a mission and that mission is death. Don't worry about life or death, you can't change what is or what will be, and the sun also rises.

## "VISTORS ON PLANET EARTH"

Visitors on planet earth, we the people indirectly gave up the gift of life for a loan and we call it life. We are afraid to call it what it is and refuse to tell anyone else, so we dream, dream, dream, hoping to bypass the inevitable, so we play, we pray and we hope to stay here on planet earth and beyond; passing this story on and on and on; not understanding that play and pray has a cousin named pay.

In conclusion, decide if you want to try and pay the loan on the road to getting back to the gift and will playing, praying and hoping get you there? Your time might be better served by accepting this loan, and understanding that a gift is a gift and the only say the receiver has is to accept it or reject it when or if it is offered.

However, you can use your loan; and if you are wise you may get an extension.

## "THE SPIRIT"

Pearl, our loss is so great that our
selfishness makes it difficult to accept,
but god understands our pain. The pain you
feel is going to need your faith and courage
to sustain you, moving on, that is what we
do when our job on earth is through, and
we are all moving on.

I know the pain of separation. This fragile body of ours can only take so much and then god releases us, so our spirit can move painlessly and freely. The spirit will never die and the physical body knows nothing. Hold on to the love between you and him and ask god to keep you strong on your journey. God wants to use us all to do his will; we come to serve and then we leave. God knows best and he took him out of his suffering.

His spirit will always be with you. He is in god's company, god is a spirit, try to think of what your husband would want you to do with the rest of your physical life? You have been a patient, long-suffering and loving wife. God is our source and Jesus is the way.

## "TIME"

Who has time? Time has time. A loan from time is what we have, we can never say we have time and be honest, because we don't have time, time has us and it always wins. I love time because time does not play favorites, it has the power to use a broad brush and get away with it and no man can stop time.

What is time? Time is one of a few things that is an equal distributor, you can't buy it, you can't sell it, you can't save it, you can't change it, when it's gone, it's gone. Time does what it wants to do, and what it wants to do is to be in control. Whoever we are or whatever we are it is the only constant that stays the course, without regard to anyone or anything.

## "ALL EXPERIENCES"

I am thankful for all of my life's experiences, it has allowed me to grow through the tears and pain, through the joy and laughter and through the lost and gain; it is almost like shedding the old skin for a newer fresher skin; life's experiences are the greatest roller coaster ride one can ever take, but when it's said and done you are mentally and emotionally stronger. Was it all worth the trip? You tell me.

## "ONE TEAR"

One tear deserves another, all tears count,
all taste of salt if I can cry why not
you? Don't say that two wrongs don't make
it right because what you are really saying
is let me get away with it, whatever it is!
Stop trying to put one over on somebody and
understand that one deed deserves another
and like it or not it will happen.

## "FRIENDSHIP"

Friends are those that give you good information tactfully, not those that either say, nothing to your face or those that go along with everything that you say. Those strong enough to take your temporary rejection and wait for you to show yourself a friend by looking at the information clearly and carefully and accepting or rejecting that information objectively as a friend.

## "BEAUTY"

It's true beauty is in the eyes of the beholder not saying we don't see physical beauty however, physical beauty is so shallow and short-lived, and in many cases misused, making it a very ugly thing in its actions. Internal beauty is eternal, it out last our physical existence. That good spirit always lives in the minds and hearts of the living. I don't think we realize or maybe we don't care enough about the pain we bring to others when we look on them and make a subjective decision on their beauty.

For example, we may say or think he or she

is so ugly or we may say

or think he or she is so beautiful

either way we are wrong. Subjective viewing

is seldom right because that kind of

viewing clouds your vision. There is

nothing wrong with looking at someone or

something you see as beautiful but, we don't

have to hurt what we don't see as beautiful

and we do ourselves a great long-term favor

by looking through what we think we see.

## "WEIGHT"

We use weight as a weapon against anyone that is not at our ideal weight as we see it. It is true that weight can be a problem to our good health however, when most people look at weight they look at the so-called over-weighted in the negative but, we need to also look at the under-weighted that can also be a serious problem. If we really want to help somebody that may have a weight problem we need to approach that person lovingly and gingerly because you need to understand that if you approach the person wrongly it will possibly cause that person to do more of what got them in the weight problem in the first place.

Whether it's an over-weight problem or an under-weight problem keep in mind that people over-eat and under-eat for many different reasons.  Some of it may be coming from biological connections, medications, a sluggish metabolism, emotional problems, poor eating habits or a combination of any and all of these things.  Get at why this behavior and you will then know how to possibly help this person.

## "LAZY"

We must always work against lazy. Lazy destroys lives and the saddest part is that the lazy self-made victim knows their condition but, is unwilling to make positive changes in their behavior, again allowing lazy to over-take their lives. When this happens the lazy self-made victim displays bitterness, jealousy and any and all other destructive behavior that they can figure out to do. They are in quick-sand and don't know it. They are blinded by their negative behavior. It is much easier to help yourself than it is to hurt yourself; while you are trying to hurt anyone else.

# "FINDING YOUR WAY"

Self-righteousness is a very dangerous
thing it has a blinding effect on your life.
Selective selfishness is unproductive.
It is as if you are stealing from yourself.
Most of this kind of behavior comes from a
loveless life, it is an unfortunate truth.
We can only give what we have; pity is the
only word to use here but, like everything
else in life, you don't have to be a victim
of your past you can rise above it and
begin changing your life for the better.

Forgive you for being you. Say to yourself I won't allow my past to steal my future over and over and mean it! Practice it, live it, and see how change makes all the difference in your life. You will have to give love before you can receive love and it is good to see that you are trying.

From someone who cares!

## "LOVE"

Love there is a difference between love and its deceiver sex.  Love exists with or without sex it's giving unselfishly, it's an unconditional function, motivation is initiated by the giver and the receiver acts and then only if it is real, all plastic behavior crumbles in this realm.  However, sex is mainly concerned with satisfying a physical genitalia need.  As long as the giver can relieve this desire for physical gratification the receiver looks at this as love in many cases.

Love withstands all things, sex withstands the moment. You can built and hold love. Sex is a continuous function that must be replenished regularly there is no way to hold on to it or save it. Life allows us few opportunities to be in love and to be sexually gratified. That is why most of us never experience what is real.

## "MONEY"

Money is a tool to be used as an exchange for something, not for someone.  Money provides us the opportunity to acquire things that have the possibility of bringing us comfort and pleasure however, it can not replace the human connection.  That is why we encounter many problems when we misuse money.

For example, too many of us feel that the more money we have the more powerful we become in every aspect of life, that is the biggest deception of money, it may have the appearance of what is real, when in fact you have been taken for a fool! Only when you mentally realize the importance of placement will you get the most that life has to offer from love and money.

## "MA-GEORGIE"

I love you now, even more than I loved you I'm hurt that you didn't love you or didn't know to love you more than you did. I needed you so much for all you could have given me and did give me. You had so much potential but, you just stubbornly refused to use it, even so I had the good to hold on too! The stories you read to us, that I can't remember but I do remember that you refused to let your light shine. You had so much to give and I really believe you didn't know what you were doing and throw it all away.

Love Margaret

## "A LISTENER"

A listener is a very important person because listening is something that we all need and respect. A speaker's words lay dormant without a listener. My father, I love my father with all of me because my father was understanding, patient and most of all a great listener and I needed that because I am a great talker. His gentleness meant so much, in the sharing of some of those same qualities in my own adult life.

Love always

## "MAMA AND DEAR"

My grandmother was a very powerful woman. She had a great influence on my life because she was a very good role model for me. She was a domestic, a midwife, a wife and a mother. She would tell me stories about her childhood and that early in her life, of her hourly duties such as, cooking and cleaning. The many different domestic jobs she had but, in particularly, of a white infant that she cared for and of how she toilet trained him before he reached his first birthday.

My grandmother was the woman that delivered all my sisters and brothers (I actually saw my baby brother being born.) My grandfather always spoke of what a lucky man he was to have my grandmother as a wife and of how hard she worked in the home with their children and outside the home. He would say "MARGET, me and your ma got a team effort." I always called my grandmother mama and I always called my grandfather dear. They were just that to me a mama and a dear.

In loving memory, MARGET

## "GRANDMA AND PAPA"

My paternal grandmother was a very interesting woman. For instance, my maternal grandmother admired my paternal grandmother's calm. She would tell me stories about how she never seemed to get excited by anything, that was interesting for her because she was an excitable soul but, she looked at and looked for positive behavior and appreciated it when she saw it.

I think I was more amazed by her attitude than I was by the stories. My paternal grandmother had a philosophy of life. "If I can't fix it, I give it to god." Papa, my paternal grandfather was a very energetic man. He lived for so long that a cousin of mine said "I thought papa would never die."
He only lost one tooth that he removed.

I love and miss them all

## "EILEEN"

Eileen, my dear sweet Eileen, you were always a "good soul", you loved your family and you never wasted your time. You always made your time count, you were a good and cherished friend and I loved you for that! You will always be in my heart. However, you are now wrapped in god's loving care you have been a good daughter and a true friend you will be missed dearly.

Au revoir

## "ROBYN"

ROBYN, you have a bunny, rabbit mentality which can be destructive. You have the ability of being great at whatever you set-out to do. However, you must work at consistency and truth, without it you sabotage your life, building your house on sand. Your words are your stamp. You need to think of your words as your identity. We label ourselves with words we do not want to diminish our words. We want to say what we mean, and mean what we say. If we do not, we not only diminish our words we lose creditability.

Lovingly MAME

## "ANN-MARIE"

Ann-Marie you have no problem climbing the
ladder of success and can and will do what
it takes to get to where you want to go.
However, be careful how you handle a fall.
It's o.k. to fall down, just get back-up,
and up, and up.  The only constant in life
is change.  Examine your choices, make a
decision and stay the course.  Sometimes you
have to cry and walk in the rain, no matter
the sun will rise, the truth will win and
your light will shine.  Be tactful, be
honest, and treat people the way you want to
be treated and take nothing less.  That's
a winning hand!

Love you
MAME

## "ARNETTA-SPECIAL"

The dictionary defines special as distinguished by some unusual quality. ARNETTA you are special. You always try to be helpful, you are a woman of few words but, you pay attention to everything that's going on around you. For instance, if somebody needs a light she will turn the light on if somebody needs a hand she will gladly give them hers. She has the insight to know when her services are needed. It's quite amazing for someone who's been labeled retarded but, it's true and that's what makes her "SOOOOO SPECIAL"! All of us have a special place, in this world and I love you!

MAME

# "ASABERRY"

For my first grandchild born August 9, 1989 the celebration of life is an awesome event it's then you know the celebration is relevant to your everlasting existence. Hello baby and welcome to the world! Mr. ASABERRY RUSSELL RAMON COLEMAN. We waited for you, and waited for you, to make your entrance on to the world, and we are so glad to see you a healthy, bouncing determined baby boy. You have grown into a fine young man that walks easy, moves steady and never misses the sun.

Love grandma

## WUNAND-"GOD IS GOOD"

Mr. MARLON ANDRE WUNAND WILLIAMS, born on November 26, 1993, my second grandchild, which makes it twice the love. MARLON you have shown determination from birth. For example, you attempted to pull the umbilical cord from around your neck, it was as if you were trying to say "not me, let me breath." MARLON you are growing-up to be a sensitive, sensible young man. I am proud to have you as a grandson, stay the course and win the race. Your humor and quick-whit is wonderful in a word. I see great things ahead for you.

Love grandma

## "A HIGHER POWER"

A higher power, it doesn't matter what you call it but, this higher power that we look on not, that we touch not, that we see not is able to show us the way of that power in our own personal lives. It is amazing that we have never been formally introduced but, inside of us we know there has to be a power greater than us, from the results of what we did not see or what we did not touch, that's power in its-self, to be able to do that! We need to show love, we need to show respect and we need to show a healthy fear of this higher power.

## **About The Author**

As a young child my mother would read to me at bedtime. I so looked forward to being in my mother's bed and having her read to me. I enjoyed that mother and daughter time "SOOO" much. Also, my maternal grandmother use to orally tell me many stories. I love stories. For instance, I use to watch a cooking show and the cook use to always tell stories. I loved the stories as much as I enjoyed the cooking. By chance, when I discovered that I could get audible books online, I was like a child so excited by it; that I even told the audible representative about my story book life.

www.ingramcontent.com/pod-product-compliance
Lightning Source LLC
Chambersburg PA
CBHW052120070526
44584CB00017B/2567